AF688187

Strategic Intelligence

Why the Future Belongs to Leaders Who Master AI Communication

by

Dr. Quannesha Trimble

Published by

Bleu Dynasty Enterprise, LLC

Atlanta, Georgia

Copyright Page

© 2026 Bleu Dynasty Enterprise, LLC. All rights reserved.

No part of this publication may be reproduced, distributed, or transmitted in any form or by any means—including photocopying, recording, scanning, or other electronic or mechanical methods—without the prior written permission of the publisher, except in the case of brief quotations used in reviews, scholarly work, or other noncommercial uses permitted by copyright law.

Strategic Intelligence: Why the Future Belongs to Those Who Master AI Communication

Author: Dr. Quannesha Trimble

Published by:

Bleu Dynasty Enterprise, LLC

Atlanta, Georgia, USA

Disclaimer

This book is for educational and informational purposes only. The strategies, frameworks, and insights presented are based on the author's professional experience and are intended to support informed decision-making. The author and publisher make no guarantees regarding specific outcomes. Readers are responsible for their own actions and results.

Trademark Notice

The T.R.A.I.N. Method™ is a proprietary strategic communication framework developed by Dr. Quannesha Trimble and owned by Bleu Dynasty Enterprise, LLC. Unauthorized use, reproduction, or distribution is strictly prohibited.

Cover design by Bleu Dynasty Enterprise, LLC

Printed in the United States of America

Dedication Page

This book is dedicated to those who choose faith over fear in the face of change.

Preface

I wrote this book to explore a connection that many people have not yet considered—the relationship between science and artificial intelligence.

My background in biological science and education taught me that complex systems operate through communication. Signals move through networks, creating coordinated responses that allow systems to function and adapt.

As I began working with artificial intelligence, I noticed something striking. Artificial intelligence responds to signals too. That realization changed the way I thought about technology, work, and the future.

But this book is not only about artificial intelligence. It is also about opportunity. One of the most important lessons life teaches us is that it is never too late to explore new paths. At any stage of life, people have the freedom to learn new skills, pivot their careers, and pursue work that truly inspires them.

Throughout history, new innovations have often caused uncertainty and debate. When something unfamiliar appears, it can create an uproar simply because the world has never encountered it before. Artificial intelligence is one of those moments. It is not going away. It is becoming part of the systems shaping our future.

The question is not whether AI will exist. The question is whether we will learn how to work with it strategically. Because the people who understand how to guide intelligent systems will have a powerful advantage in the years ahead. This book begins that conversation.

TABLE OF CONTENTS

Introduction

Something important is happening right now. Artificial intelligence is rapidly entering the systems that shape how we work, learn, create, and make decisions. Every day, new tools appear, new headlines are written, and new predictions are made about what AI will mean for the future.

Some people see opportunity. Others see uncertainty. But one thing is becoming increasingly clear: The real advantage in the AI era will not belong to those who simply experiment with the technology.

It will belong to those who learn how to communicate with intelligence itself. Most people are approaching artificial intelligence the same way they approach a search engine—typing a quick request and hoping for a useful answer.

But artificial intelligence is not just a search tool. It is something far more powerful. It is a system that responds to signals. The structure of those signals determines the quality of the outcome. This simple idea is at the heart of everything you are about to read. Because once you begin to understand how intelligence—both human and artificial—responds to communication, something remarkable happens. You stop using AI randomly. You begin guiding it strategically. And when that shift occurs, the possibilities expand dramatically.

This book is not about teaching you how to use artificial intelligence as a tool. It is about showing you how to think differently about intelligence itself. Because the future will not belong to those who fear artificial intelligence. And it will not belong to those who ignore it. The future will belong to those who learn how to guide it.

Chapter 1

The Moment Everything Changed

*

The future of work will not be decided by who has access to artificial intelligence. It will be decided by who knows how to communicate with it. Right now, millions of people are opening AI tools every day. They type a few words. They receive an answer. They close the window. And many of them walk away believing they have just experienced the full potential of artificial intelligence. But they have not. Not even close. Because the difference between average AI results and extraordinary AI results has very little to do with the software itself. It has everything to do with how the human being behind the keyboard communicates with the machine. This realization didn't come to me through technology. It came through science.

Long before artificial intelligence became part of my professional work, I spent years studying how communication works inside the human body. My academic training was rooted in biological science. I later earned a Doctorate of Chiropractic and spent time teaching Anatomy and Physiology laboratory courses for A&P I and A&P II at West Georgia Technical College. I had the privilege of guiding students through the complex systems that keep the human body functioning—muscles, nerves, organs, and the intricate networks that connect them all. When students first encounter anatomy and physiology, they often feel overwhelmed.

The body appears incredibly complicated. But eventually something remarkable happens. Patterns begin to emerge. Students realize that the body is not just a collection of parts. It is a communication system. See Visual 1: Human Communication System on the next page.

Visual 1: Human Communication System

Brain

↓

Nervous System

↓

Muscles & Organs

↓

Action

Biological systems operate through communication signals — a principle that also appears in artificial intelligence.

The brain sends instructions. The nervous system carries signals. The body responds. Movement happens. Life happens. But when those signals become disrupted or unclear, the system struggles. Communication determines function. Years later, when artificial intelligence tools began appearing in business, education, and everyday life, I started noticing something familiar. People were interacting with AI systems every day. But most of them were sending very weak signals. Short prompts. Vague instructions. Then they wondered why the responses were inconsistent. To me, it felt like watching someone try to move their arm without a signal from the brain. The system wasn't broken. The signal was incomplete. That realization changed the way I began exploring artificial intelligence. Instead of treating AI like a search engine, I approached it like a communication system. And everything changed.

The First Experiment

Like many professionals, my early interactions with artificial intelligence were simple. Curiosity. Experimentation. Testing what the technology could do. But the more I explored it, the more I noticed something interesting. Two people could use the exact same AI tool and experience completely different results. One person would say, "AI isn't that impressive." Another would say, "This technology just saved me hours of work." Same tool. Same system. Completely different outcomes. The question that fascinated me was why. My scientific training made me look for patterns. And the pattern quickly became obvious. People who communicated with AI in a structured way consistently received better results. They gave the system context. They explained the goal. They clarified the audience. They defined the outcome they wanted. In other words, they treated artificial intelligence like they would treat a highly capable assistant.

And when they did that, the quality of the output changed dramatically. This was the moment the deeper realization began to form. Artificial intelligence wasn't just a tool. It was a new layer of intelligence available to humans. But like any intelligent system, it required direction.

Intelligence Without Direction

Imagine hiring one of the most intelligent employees in the world. Someone capable of analyzing information instantly, generating ideas, and solving complex problems. Then imagine giving that employee instructions like this: "Help my business." Or: "Write something good." The employee would likely respond with confusion. Not because they lack intelligence. But because the instruction lacks clarity. Artificial intelligence works the same way.

When people say that AI gives average results, what they are often experiencing is not a limitation of the technology. It is a limitation of the instruction. Clear thinking produces clear instructions. Clear instructions produce powerful outcomes.

And that is when artificial intelligence begins to feel less like a tool and more like a thinking partner.

A New Kind of Skill

Throughout history, technological revolutions have always created new skills. The printing press made literacy powerful. The internet made digital communication essential. Artificial intelligence is introducing another skill that many people have not yet fully recognized. The skill of communicating with intelligence. Not just human intelligence. But artificial intelligence. This skill is quickly becoming one of the most valuable capabilities in the modern workforce. Not because AI replaces thinking. But because it amplifies thinking. And amplification works in both directions. Clear thinking becomes clearer. Artificial intelligence magnifies the signal we send to it.

The Emerging Divide

As artificial intelligence continues to spread across industries, a quiet divide is beginning to form. On one side are people experimenting with AI. They try prompts. They test ideas. They occasionally receive helpful outputs. On the other side are people learning to work with AI strategically. They understand that the system responds best when communication is structured. They guide the technology toward specific outcomes. They treat artificial intelligence as a collaborator in problem-solving. Over time, the gap between these two groups will grow. Not because one group has access to better technology. But because one group has learned how to communicate with intelligence.

The Beginning of Strategic Intelligence

When I began teaching professionals and organizations how to interact with artificial intelligence more effectively, I realized something important. Most people were not struggling because they lacked intelligence. They were struggling because no one had taught them how to structure the signal. Once they learned that skill, everything changed. AI responses improved. Ideas became clearer. Work that once took hours could be completed in minutes. The technology had not changed. But the communication had. And that is where the idea behind this book was born. Artificial intelligence will transform the world. But the people who benefit the most will not simply be those who use AI. They will be those who learn how to guide intelligence with intention. They will develop what I call strategic intelligence. The ability to combine human insight with artificial capability. To think clearly. To communicate precisely. And to direct powerful systems toward meaningful outcomes. Because in the end, the future will not belong to the people who fear artificial intelligence. It will belong to the people who learn how to work with it intelligently. And that journey begins with understanding the revolution we are living through.

Chapter 2

The AI Revolution Most People Misunderstand

*

Every major technological revolution begins with a misunderstanding. When electricity was first introduced, many people believed it was dangerous and unnecessary. Some cities even debated banning electric lights because they feared the technology would disrupt daily life. When the internet began expanding into homes and businesses, critics argued it was little more than a novelty—a place for hobbyists and computer enthusiasts. Today, artificial intelligence is entering a similar stage. Everyone is talking about it. Few people truly understand it. Open any news website or scroll through social media, and you will see dramatic headlines: "AI Will Replace Millions of Jobs." "Artificial Intelligence Will Transform Every Industry." "Machines Are Becoming Smarter Than Humans." The conversations surrounding artificial intelligence often swing between two extremes. Fear. Or hype. But both perspectives miss the deeper truth about what is actually happening. Artificial intelligence is not simply a technological breakthrough. It is a communication breakthrough. And most people have not realized it yet.

The Search Engine Mistake

The biggest reason people misunderstand artificial intelligence is because they approach it like a search engine. For decades, the internet trained us to interact with technology in a very specific way. You open a search bar, type a short phrase and receive links to information. The interaction is quick. Simple. But artificial intelligence does not function like a search engine. Search engines retrieve information. Artificial intelligence generates intelligence. That difference changes everything. People treat AI like Google. They type short prompts like: "Give me business ideas." "Write a social media post." "Explain artificial intelligence." The system will produce a response. Sometimes it will even be impressive. But those outputs only represent a fraction of the technology's potential. Artificial intelligence becomes significantly more powerful when the user stops treating it like a search engine and starts treating it like a collaborator. A collaborator needs direction. Context. Purpose. Clarity. Without those elements, even the most intelligent system will produce limited results. See Visual 2: Search Engine vs Artificial Intelligence on the next page.

Visual 2: Search Engine vs Artificial Intelligence

TECHNOLOGY COMPARISON

Search Engines:

- Retrieve information
- Use keyword queries
- Static results
- Designed for information lookup

Artificial Intelligence:

- Generates new intelligence
- Uses conversational interaction
- Dynamic responses
- Designed for strategic thinking

Artificial intelligence is fundamentally different from traditional search technology. While search engines retrieve information, AI systems generate structured insights.

Intelligence Is Only as Good as the Instruction

Imagine hiring one of the most intelligent employees in the world. Someone capable of analyzing vast amounts of information instantly. Someone who can draft reports, generate ideas, and solve complex problems. Now imagine giving that employee instructions like this: "Help my business." The employee would probably pause for a moment and ask: "What exactly would you like me to do?" Artificial intelligence operates in a similar way. The system is capable of extraordinary outputs, but it relies on the quality of the instruction it receives. If the instruction is vague, the output becomes vague. If the instruction is precise, the output becomes powerful. In other words, artificial intelligence reflects the clarity of human thinking. This is why two people using the same AI tool can experience dramatically different outcomes. One person may believe the technology is overrated. Another may believe it is revolutionary. The difference often comes down to one factor. Communication.

Artificial Intelligence as an Amplifier

Another misunderstanding about AI is the idea that it replaces intelligence. In reality, artificial intelligence works more like an amplifier. An amplifier does not create music. It makes the music louder. Artificial intelligence does not replace thinking. It magnifies thinking. When someone approaches AI with a clear objective, structured instructions, and thoughtful context, the system can produce outputs that feel almost extraordinary. But when someone approaches AI with vague requests and scattered thinking, the results reflect that same lack of clarity. Artificial intelligence amplifies the signal it receives. And that means the true power of AI lies not only in the technology itself, but in the human skill of directing intelligence.

A New Type of Literacy

Throughout history, technological revolutions have introduced new forms of literacy. In the early days of the printing press, literacy meant the ability to read and write. During the rise of computers, digital literacy became essential. People who could navigate software, manage files, and communicate through digital platforms gained significant advantages. Artificial intelligence is introducing another form of literacy. The ability to communicate with intelligent systems. This skill is still emerging. Few schools teach it. Few workplaces formally train employees in it. Yet it is rapidly becoming one of the most valuable capabilities in modern professional environments. Individuals who understand how to communicate effectively with AI can: Generate ideas faster. Organize complex information more efficiently. Produce high-quality work with greater speed. Solve problems with expanded analytical support. This does not mean artificial intelligence replaces human creativity. It means human creativity now has a new partner.

The Beginning of the AI Productivity Gap

As artificial intelligence spreads across industries, an important shift is beginning to emerge. Some professionals are learning how to work with AI strategically. Others are simply experimenting with it. At first, the difference may appear small. But over time, the gap becomes significant. Someone who understands how to communicate effectively with AI can accomplish in one hour what previously required several hours of manual effort. Multiply that across weeks, months, and years, and the productivity advantage becomes enormous. Organizations that learn how to integrate AI strategically will move faster. Innovate more quickly. Adapt more easily to changing environments. Those that ignore this shift will eventually struggle to keep pace. The AI revolution is not only about machines becoming smarter. It is about humans learning how to direct intelligence more effectively.

The Question That Matters Most

As artificial intelligence continues evolving, many debates will dominate headlines. Will AI replace jobs? Will machines surpass human intelligence? Will technology transform every industry? These are important questions. But there is another question that may matter even more. How will humans learn to work with intelligence itself? The individuals who answer that question early will not simply keep up with the AI revolution. They will help shape it. Because the future will not belong to people who simply use artificial intelligence. It will belong to those who learn how to communicate with it strategically. And that realization opens the door to an entirely new way of thinking about technology, work, and human potential.

Chapter 3

The AI Productivity Gap

*

Technological revolutions rarely affect everyone equally. When the internet began transforming the world in the late 1990s and early 2000s, some people saw it as little more than a digital curiosity. They used email occasionally, browsed websites, and treated the internet as a convenience rather than a strategic advantage. Others recognized something different. They realized the internet was not simply a tool— it was a new infrastructure for communication, commerce, and information. Those individuals built companies, launched platforms, and redesigned entire industries around it. The difference between the two groups was not access to the technology. Everyone had access. The difference was how they understood its potential. Today, artificial intelligence is creating a similar divide. Some people are experimenting with AI tools casually. Others are learning how to use AI strategically. And the gap between those two groups is growing rapidly.

A Quiet Divide Is Forming

At first glance, artificial intelligence appears to be available to everyone. Anyone with an internet connection can open an AI tool and begin interacting with it within seconds. This accessibility makes it seem as though the playing field is level. But in reality, something very different is happening beneath the surface. A quiet divide is forming between two types of professionals. The first group treats artificial intelligence like a digital assistant for small tasks. They ask AI to summarize information, generate quick ideas, or draft short pieces of content. These uses can certainly be helpful, but they only scratch the surface of what the technology can do. The second group approaches AI with a completely different mindset. They see artificial intelligence not simply as a tool, but as a strategic partner in thinking. They use it to explore ideas, analyze problems, organize strategies, and accelerate complex work that once required hours or days of effort. See Visual 3: The AI Productivity Gap on the next page.

Visual 3: The AI Productivity Gap

Casual AI User:

- Random prompts
- Occasional use
- Small efficiency gains
- Uses AI as a tool

Strategic AI User:

- Structured instructions
- Integrated workflow
- Exponential productivity gains
- Uses AI as a thinking partner

The gap between casual AI users and strategic AI users is already beginning to emerge.

The difference between these two approaches is enormous. And over time, it will create a productivity gap that becomes impossible to ignore.

The Research Behind the Shift

The emerging productivity advantage of artificial intelligence is not simply speculation. Researchers have already begun studying how AI affects real-world work environments. In one widely discussed study conducted by researchers at the Massachusetts Institute of Technology, professionals using generative AI tools were able to complete writing tasks 37 percent faster while also producing higher-quality outputs. Another study from Stanford University observed that customer support professionals who used AI assistance experienced productivity increases of approximately 14 percent overall, with the largest gains occurring among workers who previously struggled with efficiency. These findings reveal something important. Artificial intelligence does not only help experts. It also helps people expand their capabilities.

Workers who once struggled to organize ideas can now generate structured outlines quickly. Professionals who spent hours drafting documents can now refine high-quality drafts in minutes. The technology becomes a multiplier for human thinking. But there is a critical detail hidden inside these studies. The biggest gains did not come simply from using AI. They came from using AI effectively.

The Multiplier Effect

Imagine two professionals working on the same project. Both have access to the same artificial intelligence tools. The first person uses AI occasionally. They ask it to summarize a document or provide a few ideas. The second person integrates AI into their thinking process. They use it to brainstorm strategies, analyze information, refine communication, and accelerate decision-making. Over the course of a single day, the difference may appear small. But over the course of a year, the results become dramatic. The second professional produces more ideas, completes projects faster, and solves problems more efficiently. This is the multiplier effect of artificial intelligence. AI does not replace human intelligence. It expands it. But expansion requires direction. Without clear guidance, the technology produces average results. With structured thinking, it becomes extraordinarily powerful.

Why Most People Are Still Behind

If artificial intelligence is capable of producing such dramatic productivity improvements, why are so many people still using it in limited ways? The answer is surprisingly simple. Most people have never been taught how to work with AI strategically. When new technologies emerge, society often learns how to use them through trial and error. When the internet first appeared, people experimented with websites before learning how to build businesses online. When smartphones became popular, it took years for organizations to fully understand how mobile technology could transform their operations. Artificial intelligence is currently going through the same phase. Millions of people are experimenting with it. Very few people are being trained to use it strategically. But that will not remain true forever. As organizations begin recognizing the productivity advantages of AI, structured training will become essential. And the individuals who learn these skills early will have a significant advantage.

From AI User to AI Strategist

There is an important distinction between using artificial intelligence and thinking strategically with artificial intelligence. An AI user asks the system to perform tasks. An AI strategist collaborates with the system to expand thinking. The difference is subtle, but powerful. Instead of simply asking for answers, strategic AI users ask better questions. Instead of generating random ideas, they guide the system toward specific outcomes. Instead of relying on AI occasionally, they integrate it into their workflow. Over time, this shift transforms the relationship between human intelligence and artificial intelligence. AI stops feeling like a novelty. It starts functioning as a thinking partner.

The Opportunity Ahead

The AI productivity gap is still in its early stages. Most professionals have not yet realized how dramatically artificial intelligence can change the way work is done. But that will change quickly. Organizations that understand how to guide artificial intelligence effectively will move faster, innovate more rapidly, and solve problems with greater efficiency. Individuals who learn these skills will become more valuable in the workforce. Not because machines are replacing people. But because people who know how to work with intelligent systems will become the most capable problem-solvers in the room. The AI revolution is not simply about machines becoming more intelligent. It is about humans learning how to direct intelligence itself.

And that realization leads to an important question. Why do some people instinctively understand how to work with complex systems while others struggle? The answer may lie in an unexpected place. Science.

Chapter 4

Why Scientists Understand AI Differently

*

The first time many students walk into an Anatomy and Physiology laboratory, they expect to memorize facts. They expect to study diagrams of bones, muscles, organs, and nerves. But what surprises them most is that anatomy is not really about memorization. It is about systems. In the laboratory, students quickly learn that nothing in the human body operates alone. Muscles depend on nerves. Nerves depend on signals from the brain. Organs rely on networks of communication that coordinate thousands of processes every second. What appears to be a collection of individual parts is actually a highly integrated system. And once students begin to understand the body this way, everything changes. Instead of memorizing structures, they start recognizing patterns. Instead of isolated facts, they begin seeing relationships. This shift—from parts to systems—is one of the most important ways scientists learn to think. It is also one of the most powerful ways to understand artificial intelligence.

The Language of Systems

Science teaches us that complex systems are built on communication. Inside the human body, communication occurs through electrical and chemical signals. The brain sends instructions. The nervous system carries those instructions through networks of neurons. Muscles respond. Organs adjust. Information moves continuously through the system. If those signals are disrupted, the body struggles. Movement becomes difficult. Processes slow down. Coordination breaks down.

But when communication flows clearly, the system functions remarkably well. The human body is not simply a machine. It is a communication network. And in many ways, artificial intelligence works in a surprisingly similar way.

Neural Networks and the Nervous System

Modern artificial intelligence systems are built using structures known as neural networks.

The name is not accidental. Neural networks are inspired by the way neurons communicate in the human brain. In biological systems, neurons transmit signals through electrical impulses and chemical neurotransmitters. Each neuron connects to others, forming vast communication pathways that allow the brain to process information and generate responses. Artificial neural networks operate on a similar principle. Instead of biological neurons, they use mathematical nodes that process information and pass signals to other nodes within the network. Data enters the system. Patterns are analyzed. Outputs are generated. Although artificial neural networks are far simpler than the human brain, the underlying concept is similar. Information flows through a system. Signals trigger responses. Patterns emerge. The intelligence of the system depends on how information moves through these pathways. And just like in the human body, the quality of the signal matters. See Visual 4: Biological Intelligence vs. Artificial Intelligence below.

Visual 4: Biological Intelligence vs. Artificial Intelligence

```
Human Brain      Artificial Intelligence
  ↓                ↓
Neurons          Neural Network
  ↓                ↓
Nervous System   Data Processing
  ↓                ↓
Human Response   AI Output
```

Artificial neural networks were inspired by biological communication systems.

Signals Shape the Outcome

In Anatomy and Physiology, one of the most important lessons students learn is that the body responds to signals. If a signal tells a muscle to contract, the muscle contracts. If the signal is disrupted, the muscle cannot respond correctly. The system behaves according to the information it receives. Artificial intelligence behaves in much the same way. The output produced by AI systems depends heavily on the instructions they receive. When the input is vague or incomplete, the response may be general or unfocused. When the input is clear and structured, the system produces more refined results. In other words, artificial intelligence reflects the signal it receives. This principle is one of the most important insights professionals can understand about AI. The technology is powerful. But the communication directing that technology is even more important.

Systems Thinking in the Age of AI

People trained in scientific disciplines often develop a skill known as systems thinking. Systems thinking means understanding how individual parts interact within a larger structure. Instead of analyzing isolated components, systems thinkers look for relationships. They ask questions such as: How does this part affect the rest of the system? What signals are moving through this network? Where are the communication pathways? This type of thinking becomes incredibly valuable when working with artificial intelligence. AI systems are not simple tools. They are information systems. They analyze patterns, process signals, and generate responses based on structured input. The more clearly someone understands how these systems operate, the more effectively they can guide them. And that is where a new kind of skill begins to emerge.

The Emergence of Strategic Communication

As artificial intelligence becomes integrated into everyday work, a surprising realization is beginning to surface. The most important skill in the AI era may not be coding. It may not be programming. It may not even be technical expertise. The most important skill may be the ability to communicate with intelligent systems. This is where many professionals are still learning. They approach AI casually. They type a short request. They accept whatever answer appears. But those who understand systems begin approaching AI differently. They recognize that artificial intelligence responds to structured communication. They guide the system with intention. They refine instructions. They shape the signal. Over time, this shift produces dramatically better outcomes. Artificial intelligence becomes less like a tool and more like a collaborative system.

The Advantage of Seeing Patterns

When scientists study complex systems, they look for patterns that explain behavior. Biologists study patterns in ecosystems. Physiologists study patterns in body systems. Neuroscientists study patterns in brain activity. Artificial intelligence operates through patterns as well. AI models analyze enormous amounts of data to identify relationships between words, ideas, and concepts. When you interact with an AI system, you are essentially guiding a pattern-recognition engine. The system predicts what information should come next based on the signals you provide. This is why communication with AI matters so much. The clearer the pattern in your instructions, the clearer the pattern in the output. Once people understand this concept, their interaction with AI changes dramatically. They stop asking vague questions. They start crafting intentional signals. And the system responds accordingly.

The Bridge Between Biology and Artificial Intelligence

For me, the connection between biological systems and artificial intelligence was impossible to ignore. Both depend on signals. Both operate through networks. Both generate responses based on patterns of information. The more I explored this connection, the more I realized that many professionals were approaching AI without understanding the systems behind it. They were interacting with the technology without understanding the communication principles that made it work. Once those principles became clear, the technology became far more powerful. Artificial intelligence stopped feeling mysterious. It began to feel logical. And when something becomes logical, it becomes learnable.

The Beginning of a New Skill

The ability to communicate effectively with artificial intelligence is still a relatively new skill. Most people have not been formally taught how to do it. Yet it is rapidly becoming one of the most valuable capabilities in modern work environments. Organizations are beginning to recognize that AI tools alone do not create transformation. Strategy creates transformation. And strategy begins with communication. The professionals who learn how to guide artificial intelligence will gain a powerful advantage. They will solve problems faster. Generate ideas more efficiently. And collaborate with intelligent systems in ways that expand their own capabilities. But this raises an important question. If communication is the key to unlocking the power of AI, how exactly should that communication be structured? The answer lies in a principle that sits at the center of strategic intelligence. And understanding that principle is what turns artificial intelligence from a curiosity into a competitive advantage.

Chapter 5

The Strategic Communication Advantage

*

Throughout history, the people who learned how to communicate with powerful systems early gained extraordinary advantages. When the printing press transformed the spread of information, literacy became one of the most valuable skills a person could possess. When computers entered the workplace, those who understood how to interact with software gained enormous professional advantages. When the internet connected the world, individuals who understood digital communication reshaped industries. Today, artificial intelligence is introducing another shift. And once again, the advantage belongs to those who understand how to communicate with the system. Not casually. Not randomly. But strategically.

The Difference Between Using AI and Directing AI

Many professionals today are using artificial intelligence. But very few are directing it. There is a significant difference between these two approaches. An AI user opens a tool and asks for something. An AI strategist guides the system toward a specific outcome. This difference may seem subtle, but it changes the entire interaction. Consider the difference between these two instructions: "Write something about leadership." Versus: "Write a short article explaining why strategic thinking will become one of the most valuable leadership skills in the AI era. The audience is business executives, and the tone should be insightful and professional." The first instruction is vague. The second instruction provides context, direction, and purpose. Artificial intelligence performs dramatically better when communication is structured this way. And once people begin interacting with AI at this level of clarity, something remarkable happens. The technology becomes far more useful. Ideas become more refined. Work becomes faster. Artificial intelligence stops feeling like a novelty. It begins to feel like a thinking partner.

Why Structure Changes Everything

Structured communication works because it mirrors how intelligent systems process information. Inside the human brain, signals move through networks of neurons in highly organized patterns. Those signals determine how information is processed and how responses are generated. Artificial intelligence systems operate through similar patterns. When the input is organized, the system can interpret it more effectively. When the input lacks clarity, the output becomes less precise. This is why professionals who learn how to structure their communication with AI consistently receive better results. They are not simply using the technology. They are guiding it. They understand that artificial intelligence performs best when it receives clear signals about: purpose, context, audience, and outcome. Once these elements are present, the system becomes significantly more capable.

A New Kind of Professional Skill

As artificial intelligence becomes embedded in more industries, a new professional skill is emerging. The ability to communicate strategically with intelligent systems. This skill is not limited to programmers or engineers. In fact, it may become even more valuable for people working in fields such as: business strategy, marketing, education, consulting, healthcare, and entrepreneurship. These professionals often rely on the ability to generate ideas, analyze information, and communicate clearly. Artificial intelligence can support all of these activities—but only when it receives well-structured instructions. In this way, the relationship between humans and artificial intelligence begins to resemble a partnership. The human provides direction. The AI provides computational power and pattern recognition. Together, they create results that neither could achieve alone.

The Emergence of Strategic Intelligence

As I began working with entrepreneurs, professionals, and organizations exploring artificial intelligence, I noticed a consistent pattern. Many people were curious about AI. Few understood how to guide it effectively. They would ask general questions. They would experiment with short prompts. Sometimes they would receive impressive responses. Other times they would receive results that felt incomplete or generic. But once they learned how to structure their communication with AI, the experience changed dramatically. The system began producing more focused ideas. Strategies became clearer. Workflows became faster. This shift represented something deeper than simply learning how to use a new tool. It represented the development of a new type of thinking. A form of intelligence that combines human insight with artificial capability. I began referring to this skill as strategic intelligence. The ability to guide powerful systems through structured communication. The ability to transform artificial intelligence from a passive tool into an active collaborator. And the more I observed this transformation, the more I realized that this skill would become one of the defining capabilities of the AI era.

The Principle Behind the Method

Over time, my work helping professionals interact more effectively with artificial intelligence led me to develop a structured communication model designed to guide AI systems toward meaningful outcomes. See Visual 5: The T.R.A.I.N.™ Strategic Intelligence Model on the next page.

Visual 5: The T.R.A.I.N. Model

A Strategic Framework for Communicating with Artificial Intelligence

- T – Tell the role
- R – Refine the context
- A – Add constraints
- I – Instruct format
- N – Narrow the goal

The T.R.A.I.N. Framework developed by Dr. Quannesha Trimble is a strategic communication model designed to guide artificial intelligence toward high-quality outcomes. The complete methodology is taught in Dr. Trimble's advanced AI strategy training programs.

This model provides a framework for thinking about how instructions should be structured when interacting with artificial intelligence. Because this framework forms the foundation of my professional consulting and training programs, the full methodology is taught in greater depth within those environments. However, the underlying principle is simple. Artificial intelligence performs best when communication is intentional. When the signal is structured. When the objective is clear. When the direction is thoughtful. This principle may seem obvious once understood. Yet it is surprisingly rare in practice. Most people approach artificial intelligence the same way they approach a search engine—briefly and casually. Strategic AI users approach it differently. They recognize that the quality of the signal determines the quality of the outcome.

The Strategic Advantage

As artificial intelligence continues spreading across industries, the ability to communicate with intelligent systems will become increasingly valuable. Organizations that understand this skill will move faster. Innovate more effectively. Solve complex problems with greater efficiency. Individuals who master this skill will find themselves operating at a different level of productivity. Not because they are working harder. But because they are working with intelligence. This is the true advantage of artificial intelligence. It does not eliminate human creativity. It expands it. It does not replace strategic thinking. It amplifies it. And the individuals who learn how to guide these systems early will shape the future of how work is done.

A Turning Point

At this stage in the story of artificial intelligence, we are standing at an important turning point. The technology is becoming more powerful every year. New capabilities are emerging at a pace few people predicted. But the most important transformation may not occur within the technology itself. It may occur within the people who learn how to use it strategically. The professionals who learn how to communicate with artificial intelligence will unlock possibilities that once required entire teams, departments, or organizations. And those possibilities will reshape how we think about work, creativity, and human potential. But to fully understand where this transformation is heading, we must explore the broader impact artificial intelligence will have on the future of work. Because the skills that define success today may look very different in the years ahead.

Chapter 6

Human Intelligence + Artificial Intelligence

*

Every time a powerful new technology appears, the same question eventually emerges. Will this replace us? When machines were first introduced into factories during the Industrial Revolution, workers feared automation would eliminate human labor entirely. When computers entered offices decades later, professionals worried that software would make many jobs obsolete. Today, artificial intelligence has sparked the same conversation. Will AI replace humans? The question is understandable. Artificial intelligence systems can now generate text, analyze data, write code, summarize research, and assist with complex decision-making tasks. At first glance, it can seem as though machines are beginning to take over roles once performed exclusively by people. But history tells us something important about technological revolutions. The technologies that transform society most dramatically rarely eliminate human capability. Instead, they expand it. Artificial intelligence is no exception.

The Real Transformation

The real transformation taking place today is not the replacement of human intelligence. It is the expansion of it. Artificial intelligence allows humans to interact with information in ways that were previously impossible. A professional working alone can now analyze data that once required teams of analysts. An entrepreneur can generate strategic ideas at a pace that once required extensive brainstorming sessions. Educators can create learning materials more quickly.

Researchers can explore information faster. Artificial intelligence is not removing the human from the process. It is increasing what a single human mind can accomplish. This is why the future will not belong to machines. It will belong to people who learn how to work with

machines intelligently.

The Partnership Model

One of the most helpful ways to understand artificial intelligence is to think of it as a partnership. Humans and AI each bring unique strengths to the collaboration. Humans excel at: creativity, intuition, strategic, thinking, ethical judgment, and vision. Artificial intelligence excels at: pattern recognition, data processing, speed, information retrieval and structuring ideas. When these strengths combine, the result is far more powerful than either could achieve alone. A human mind guided by creativity and purpose can direct an AI system capable of processing enormous amounts of information. Together, they create something new. A collaborative intelligence. See Visual 6: Human + AI Collaboration Model on the next page.

Visual: 6 Human + AI Collaboration Model

Human + AI Collaboration Model

Human Creativity

+

Strategic Thinking

+

Artificial Intelligence

=

Strategic Intelligence

The most powerful results emerge when human insight collaborates with artificial intelligence.

The Augmented Professional

In the coming years, the most effective professionals will not simply rely on their individual expertise. They will become augmented professionals. Individuals whose capabilities are expanded through intelligent systems. Consider a consultant developing a strategy for a client. Instead of spending days manually organizing research and drafting frameworks, that consultant can now collaborate with artificial intelligence to explore multiple ideas quickly. The human provides the insight. The AI accelerates the analysis. The result is not a replacement of the consultant's expertise. It is an amplification of it. The same pattern will appear across many fields. Writers will collaborate with AI to refine ideas. Educators will design lessons with AI-supported tools. Entrepreneurs will test strategies faster. Scientists will analyze complex datasets more efficiently. In each case, artificial intelligence becomes a partner in the thinking process.

The Myth of Replacement

Much of the fear surrounding artificial intelligence comes from the belief that machines will replace human thinking entirely. But this perspective misunderstands how intelligence actually works. Machines process information. Humans assign meaning. Machines recognize patterns. Humans create purpose. Machines generate possibilities. Humans decide which possibilities matter. Artificial intelligence can assist with many tasks, but it does not replace the deeper human abilities that shape innovation, leadership, and vision. Instead, it extends the reach of those abilities. It gives individuals the ability to explore ideas faster and develop solutions more efficiently. In this sense, artificial intelligence acts less like a competitor and more like an intellectual multiplier.

The Leaders of the AI Era

Because artificial intelligence amplifies human capability, the individuals who benefit most from AI will not necessarily be the most technical people. They will be the most strategic thinkers. The leaders who thrive in the AI era will possess a combination of abilities. They will understand: how to ask meaningful questions, how to guide, intelligent systems, how to interpret information and how to apply insights creatively. These abilities allow humans to direct artificial intelligence rather than simply react to it. In other words, the most successful professionals of the future will not simply be AI users. They will be AI strategists.

A New Kind of Collaboration

The collaboration between human intelligence and artificial intelligence is still in its early stages. The tools available today are only the beginning. In the coming years, AI systems will become more integrated into everyday work environments. They will assist with planning, research, communication, and decision-making. But even as these systems grow more advanced, one principle will remain constant. Artificial intelligence requires human direction. It requires someone to define the goal, interpret the outcome, and apply the insight to real-world situations. The most powerful outcomes will always come from collaboration. From humans guiding intelligent systems toward meaningful objectives. This is the essence of strategic intelligence.

Expanding Human Potential

Throughout history, humans have developed tools that extend their physical capabilities. We created machines that allow us to travel faster than our bodies alone could move. We invented devices that allow us to communicate across the globe instantly. Artificial intelligence represents something different. It extends not only our physical abilities, but our cognitive reach. It allows individuals to explore ideas more rapidly, analyze information more effectively, and organize knowledge in ways that accelerate learning. The result is not a diminished role for human intelligence. It is an expanded one. People who learn how to work with artificial intelligence gain access to a new level of capability. They become more adaptable. More innovative. More efficient. And these advantages will shape the future workforce.

The Turning Point

Artificial intelligence is still evolving. New tools appear every year. Capabilities improve. Applications expand. But the most important shift will not be technological. It will be human. The moment professionals begin seeing artificial intelligence not as a replacement, but as a partner, everything changes. Fear turns into curiosity. Curiosity turns into experimentation. Experimentation turns into mastery. And mastery leads to transformation. The individuals who understand this shift early will help define the next generation of leadership. But to understand exactly how dramatically this transformation will reshape industries, we must look ahead. Because the workplace of the next decade will look very different from the one we know today.

Chapter 7

The Future of Work in the Age of AI

*

Every generation believes it is living through a period of change. But occasionally, history produces moments where change accelerates so rapidly that entire systems must adapt. We are living in one of those moments now. Artificial intelligence is not simply introducing new tools into the workplace. It is changing the relationship between humans and information. For centuries, progress has largely been driven by human labor and human knowledge. Organizations relied on teams of people to gather data, analyze information, develop strategies, and execute ideas. Artificial intelligence is beginning to alter that dynamic. Tasks that once required hours of research can now be performed in minutes. Large volumes of information can be analyzed almost instantly. Ideas can be explored at a pace that was previously impossible. This does not mean the human role in work is disappearing. It means the nature of work itself is evolving.

The Shift from Knowledge to Strategy

For much of the modern era, professional success was tied closely to knowledge. The individuals who possessed specialized information often held the greatest influence within organizations. Doctors, engineers, lawyers, analysts, and consultants-built careers around their expertise and the depth of their knowledge. But artificial intelligence is changing how knowledge functions in the workplace. Information is becoming increasingly accessible. AI systems can summarize research, analyze data, and generate explanations within seconds. As a result, the advantage of simply having information is beginning to diminish. The advantage is shifting toward something else. Strategic thinking. In an environment where information is abundant, the most valuable skill becomes the ability to interpret that information, guide intelligent systems, and apply insights effectively. This is why the future workforce will place greater emphasis on individuals who can: ask meaningful questions, identify patterns, direct intelligent systems, and translate insights into action. In other words, the future will belong to strategic thinkers.

The Rise of the AI-Augmented Professional

As artificial intelligence becomes more integrated into everyday workflows, a new type of professional is beginning to emerge. The AI-augmented professional. These individuals do not rely solely on their own cognitive capacity. Instead, they combine their expertise with the computational power of artificial intelligence. Imagine a business strategist exploring market opportunities. With AI assistance, they can analyze industry trends, review competitor strategies, and generate multiple strategic scenarios in a fraction of the time traditional research would require. The strategist still provides the judgment and decision-making. But the process of gathering and organizing information becomes dramatically faster. This pattern will appear across industries. Writers will collaborate with AI to refine ideas. Educators will design curriculum with AI-supported tools. Healthcare professionals will analyze patient data more efficiently. Entrepreneurs will test new concepts more rapidly. In each case, the professional becomes more capable because artificial intelligence expands their reach.

Industries on the Edge of Transformation

While artificial intelligence will affect nearly every field, some industries are likely to experience particularly rapid transformation. Healthcare will benefit from AI-assisted diagnostics and research analysis. Education will see the rise of personalized learning experiences tailored to individual students. Finance will use intelligent systems to analyze markets and detect patterns in economic behavior. Marketing will evolve through AI-generated insights into consumer behavior. Legal professionals will increasingly rely on AI tools to analyze documents and research case law. Entrepreneurship will become more accessible as AI assists with planning, strategy, and operational decisions. These changes will not happen overnight. But they are already beginning. The organizations that learn how to guide artificial intelligence effectively will move ahead of those that do not.

The Skills That Will Matter Most

As the nature of work evolves, certain skills will become increasingly valuable. Technical expertise will still matter. But it will not be enough on its own. The professionals who thrive in the AI era will combine technical capability with broader strategic skills. Among the most important will be: critical thinking, creative problem solving, adaptability, clear communication, and systems thinking. These abilities allow individuals to interact effectively with intelligent systems. They enable professionals to translate AI-generated insights into real-world action. And they help organizations navigate a rapidly changing technological landscape. See Visual 7: Skills of the AI-Era Leader on the next page.

Visual 7: Skills of the AI-Era Leader

SKILLS OF THE AI-ERA LEADER

Critical Thinking

+

Creative Problem Solving

+

Clear Communication

+

Systems Thinking

+

AI Collaboration

=

Future-Ready Leadership

The leaders who thrive in the AI era will combine human insight with the ability to guide intelligent systems.

The Strategic Intelligence Advantage

At the center of this transformation lies a simple idea. Artificial intelligence expands human capability. But expansion requires direction. Without clear guidance, the technology produces limited results. With strategic communication, it becomes extraordinarily powerful. This is why the ability to communicate effectively with artificial intelligence will become one of the defining professional skills of the next decade. Those who master this skill will operate at a different level of productivity. They will generate ideas faster. Solve problems more efficiently. And lead organizations through increasingly complex environments. They will possess what we might call strategic intelligence. The ability to combine human insight with artificial capability.

A Workforce in Transition

As artificial intelligence continues to evolve, the workplace will likely undergo several stages of transformation. At first, AI will assist with individual tasks. Later, it will become integrated into larger workflows. Eventually, organizations will redesign entire processes around intelligent systems. This transition will not eliminate the need for human leadership. In fact, it may increase it. The more powerful technology becomes, the more important it is to have thoughtful leaders guiding how that technology is used. The future workplace will not simply need people who understand AI. It will need people who understand how to guide intelligence responsibly and strategically.

Looking Ahead

The transformation of work will not occur overnight. But the trajectory is clear. Artificial intelligence will continue to expand its capabilities. Organizations will integrate it more deeply into operations. Professionals will learn new ways to collaborate with intelligent systems. And over time, the individuals who thrive in this environment will share one common characteristic. They will not view artificial intelligence as a replacement. They will view it as a partner. A powerful system capable of expanding what human beings can accomplish.

Understanding this partnership is essential for anyone hoping to navigate the future of work. But to fully appreciate the significance of this moment, we must take one final step. We must consider what it means to live in an era where intelligence itself is becoming a collaborative process. Because that realization marks the beginning of something new. The Strategic Intelligence Era.

Chapter 8

The Strategic Intelligence Era

*

Every era in human history has been defined by a breakthrough that changed how people live, work, and think. The Industrial Age transformed physical labor. Machines allowed humans to produce goods at a scale that had never been possible before. The Information Age transformed access to knowledge. Computers and the internet connected the world, placing vast amounts of information at our fingertips. Today, we are entering something different. A new era defined not by machines alone, and not by information alone, but by intelligence itself. Artificial intelligence is introducing a shift in how humans interact with knowledge, creativity, and problem-solving.

For the first time in history, individuals have access to systems capable of generating ideas, analyzing patterns, and assisting with complex thinking tasks But as powerful as these systems are, they do not replace human intelligence.

They expand it. And that expansion marks the beginning of what we can call the Strategic Intelligence Era.

From Tools to Intelligence

For centuries, humans have developed tools to extend their physical abilities. We built machines to move faster than we could run. We created devices to lift heavier objects than our bodies could carry. These technologies expanded our physical reach. Artificial intelligence expands something different. It expands our cognitive reach. AI systems allow humans to explore ideas more rapidly, analyze information more efficiently, and generate solutions at a pace that would once have required entire teams of experts. But like any powerful tool, intelligence amplification must be guided. Without direction, even the most advanced technology produces limited results. With strategic communication, the technology becomes transformative.

The Leaders Who Will Shape the Future

As artificial intelligence becomes embedded in organizations, industries, and everyday life, the leaders who rise to prominence will share a particular mindset. They will not simply adopt new technologies. They will learn how to direct them thoughtfully. The leaders of the Strategic Intelligence Era will understand that the value of AI lies not only in the technology itself, but in the way humans interact with it. They will ask better questions. They will structure problems more clearly. They will guide intelligent systems toward meaningful outcomes. And by doing so, they will unlock possibilities that were once unimaginable. These individuals will not compete with artificial intelligence. They will collaborate with it.

Intelligence as a Partnership

The idea that intelligence can be collaborative may feel unfamiliar at first. For much of history, intelligence has been viewed as something contained within the human mind. But artificial intelligence introduces a new model. One where humans and intelligent systems work together to solve problems. In this model, the human mind provides vision, judgment, and creativity. The AI system provides speed, pattern recognition, and analytical support. Together, they create a partnership capable of addressing challenges with greater efficiency and insight. This partnership does not diminish human capability. It magnifies it.

The Responsibility of Intelligence

As powerful technologies emerge, they always bring new responsibilities. Artificial intelligence is no exception. The ability to guide intelligent systems requires thoughtful leadership.

It requires individuals who understand not only what technology can do, but also how it should be used. Ethics, judgment, and human values remain essential components of decision-making. Artificial intelligence may assist with analysis and insight, but it is humans who ultimately decide how those insights are applied. The Strategic Intelligence Era therefore requires more than technological skill. It requires wisdom. Leaders who can balance innovation with responsibility. Curiosity with caution. Speed with thoughtful reflection.

A New Opportunity for Human Potential

Although discussions about artificial intelligence often focus on disruption, they should also focus on opportunity.

Throughout history, technological progress has expanded what humans are capable of achieving. Artificial intelligence continues that tradition. By reducing the time required to analyze information and explore ideas, AI allows individuals to focus more energy on creativity, strategy, and innovation. Entrepreneurs can develop new concepts faster. Educators can reach students in more personalized ways. Researchers can explore scientific questions more efficiently. Professionals across industries can collaborate with intelligent systems to solve problems that once seemed overwhelming. In this sense, artificial intelligence does not narrow the scope of human potential. It broadens it.

The Choice Before Us

As society enters this new era, each individual faces an important choice. We can view artificial intelligence with uncertainty and hesitation. Or we can approach it with curiosity and intention. The difference between those two perspectives will shape the future of work, leadership, and innovation. Those who resist change may find themselves struggling to adapt. Those who explore the possibilities of intelligent collaboration will discover new ways to think, create, and lead. The Strategic Intelligence Era belongs to those who choose the second path. Those who learn how to communicate with intelligence. Those who guide powerful systems toward meaningful goals. Those who recognize that the future is not something that simply happens to us. It is something we help create.

The Journey Forward

The ideas explored in this book represent the beginning of a larger journey. Artificial intelligence will continue evolving. New tools will appear. New capabilities will emerge. But the most important development will not be the technology itself. It will be the people who learn how to use that technology wisely. The professionals who understand how to communicate with artificial intelligence will gain access to a powerful new dimension of thinking. They will become architects of ideas. Designers of strategy. Leaders capable of navigating an increasingly complex world. In short, they will become practitioners of strategic intelligence.

Chapter 9

From Prompting to Power — Using the TRAIN Method™ in Your Daily Execution

*

Up to this point, you've seen the TRAIN Method™ as a simple

framework:

- T
- R
- A
- I
- N

Now it's time to bring it to life. Each letter represents a key part of how you communicate with AI:

- T — Role
- R — Context

- A — Constraints
- I — Format
- N — Goal

What you're about to see is how this simple structure transforms the way you give instructions. Each example starts with a basic, everyday prompt and then evolves into a clear, strategic command using the TRAIN Method™. This is where the shift happens—from typing requests to directing outcomes.

The T.R.A.I.N Method™ Prompt System

The following examples are built using the T.R.A.I.N Method™ Prompt System. Each one takes a basic idea and transforms it into a structured, results-driven prompt you can use immediately.

FROM GENERIC → STRATEGIC

This is where everything changes.

1. SOCIAL MEDIA (VISIBILITY → CONVERSION)

❌ Generic Prompt

"Write a social media post about my program."

T.R.A.I.N Method™ Prompt System

Act as a social media strategist for mission-driven brands. Create a high-converting Instagram caption.

Program: [INSERT PROGRAM NAME]

Audience: [WHO YOU SERVE]

Goal: Increase engagement and sign-ups

Requirements:

- Start with a strong emotional hook
- Highlight a key pain point
- Show transformation or benefit

- Keep under 150 words
- Include a clear call-to-action
- Add 5 relevant hashtags

Format: Caption + CTA + Hashtags

FROM GENERIC → STRATEGIC

2. DONOR EMAIL (ASKING → INFLUENCING)

❌ Generic Prompt

"Write a donor email."

T.R.A.I.N Method™ Prompt System

Act as a nonprofit fundraising strategist. Write a compelling donor email.

Organization Name: [INSERT]

Mission: [INSERT]

Campaign Purpose: [WHAT YOU ARE FUNDRAISING FOR]

Audience: [NEW OR EXISTING DONORS]

Requirements:

- Open with an emotional hook
- Clearly explain urgency

- Show specific impact of the donation
- Keep under 200 words
- Include a strong call-to-action

Goal: Increase donations and deepen emotional connection

FROM GENERIC → STRATEGIC

3. BUSINESS STRATEGY (CONFUSION → CLARITY)

❌ Generic Prompt

"Help me grow my business."

T.R.A.I.N Method™ Prompt System

Act as a senior business strategist. Analyze my business and provide a clear growth strategy.

Business Type: [INSERT]

Current Offers: [LIST PRODUCTS + PRICES]

Target Audience: [INSERT]

Current Challenges:

[LIST YOUR PROBLEMS]

Requirements:

- Identify top 3 growth bottlenecks
- Recommend revenue strategies

- Suggest improvements to pricing or funnel
- Include one quick win and one long-term strategy

Format:

1. Key Problems
2. Strategic Recommendations
3. Action Steps

FROM GENERIC → STRATEGIC

4. PROGRAM CREATION (IDEAS → STRUCTURE)

❌ Generic Prompt

"Create a program outline."

T.R.A.I.N Method™ Prompt System

Act as a program development expert. Design a structured program.

Program Name: [INSERT]

Target Audience: [INSERT]

Primary Goal: [TRANSFORMATION]

Key Topics: [LIST]

Provide:

- Weekly or module breakdown
- Learning objectives
- Suggested activities
- Measurable outcomes
- Final transformation result

FROM GENERIC → STRATEGIC

5. CONTENT PLANNING (INCONSISTENCY → SYSTEM)

❌ Generic Prompt

"Give me content ideas."

Act as a social media strategist. Create a 30-day content plan.

Organization/Brand: [INSERT]

Audience: [INSERT]

Goal: [AWARENESS / ENGAGEMENT / SALES]

Include:

- Daily content themes
- Caption ideas
- Call-to-action suggestions
- Mix of educational, storytelling, and promotional content

Format:

Table with Date | Topic | Caption Idea | CTA

Chapter 10

Execution Is The Difference

*

READY TO GO FROM INFORMATION TO EXECUTION?

Most people will read this book, feel inspired—and go back to doing things the same way. That's not you.

You've seen what's possible:

- Turning vague ideas into clear direction
- Replacing random prompts with structured execution
- Moving from wasted time to focused productivity

But here's the truth: Information doesn't create results. Execution does. And execution requires structure.

INTRODUCING:

AI Mastery Course

This is where strategy becomes implementation. Inside this program, you'll learn:

- The complete TRAIN Method™ execution system
- How to create high-level prompts that produce real results
- How to build your AI Command Center
- How to train AI to match your exact voice and brand
- How to apply AI across marketing, operations, and growth

This is not theory.

This is execution.

If you're ready to:

- Stop guessing with AI
- Build systems that save time and increase impact
- Operate like a strategist—not a beginner

Then this is your next step.

Enroll now

https://ai.bleudynastyenterprise.com

You were not meant to operate overwhelmed. You were meant to lead.

— Dr. Quannesha Trimble

Bleu Dynasty Enterprise, LLC

About the Author

*

Dr. Quannesha Trimble is a Certified AI Consultant and the founder of Bleu Dynasty Enterprise, LLC, where she helps entrepreneurs, professionals, and organizations transform artificial intelligence into structured, results-driven systems.

With a foundation in biological science and research, Dr. Trimble approaches AI differently. She doesn't teach people to use AI randomly—she teaches them how to communicate with it strategically.

She is the creator of the T.R.A.I.N. Method™, a proprietary framework designed to turn vague ideas into clear direction, and inconsistent outputs into high-level execution.

Through her work, she has helped individuals and organizations move from confusion to clarity, from scattered efforts to structured systems, and from information overload to strategic execution.

Her approach is simple:

AI is not the advantage.

How you use it is.

If you're ready to operate at a higher level and turn strategy into execution, you can learn more and take the next step here:

https://ai.bleudynastyenterprise.com

— Dr. Quannesha Trimble

Bleu Dynasty Enterprise, LLC

www.ingramcontent.com/pod-product-compliance
Lightning Source LLC
LaVergne TN
LVHW022016200926
848481LV00007B/2423